BIRTHDAY SQUIGGLES & SCRIBBLES

Starter squiggles & Coloring pages

DENISE HARTZLER

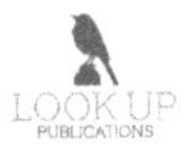

LOOK UP
PUBLICATIONS

Published by Look Up Publications, LLC in 2023
First Edition; First Printing

Design, Cover, and Writing © 2023 Denise Hartzler

www.denisehartzler.com/www.lookuppublications.com

ISBN: 978-1-7346070-4-8

DEDICATION

This book is dedicated to

YOU

on your birthday!

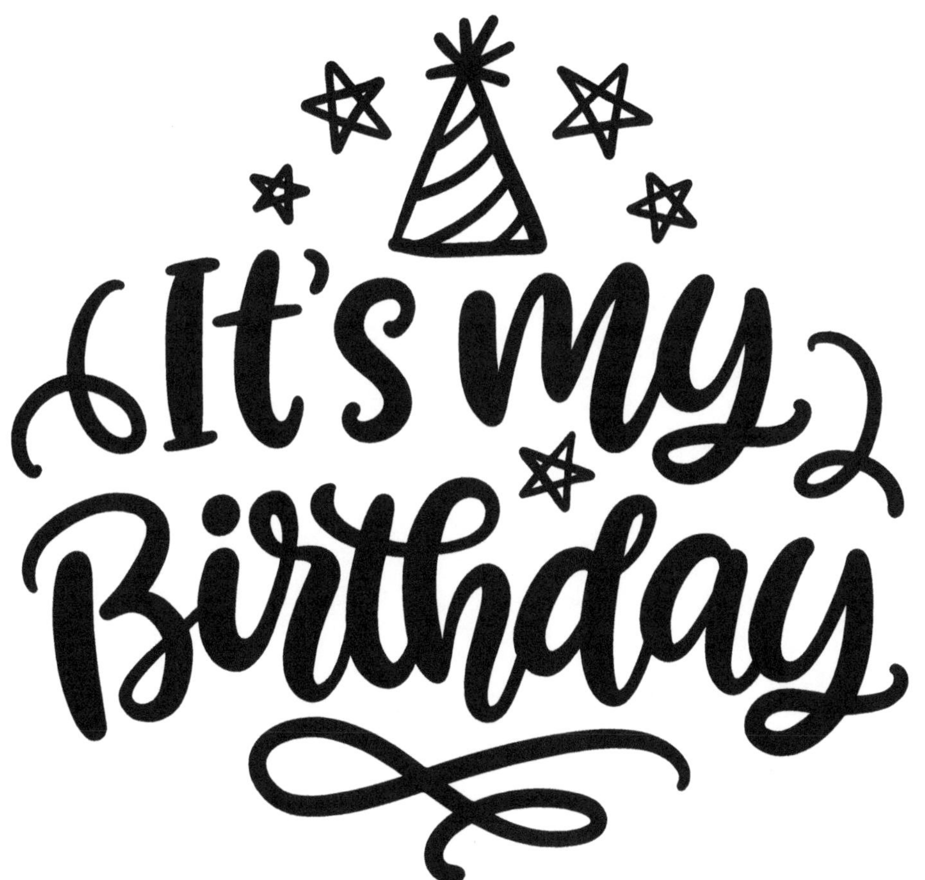
It's my
Birthday

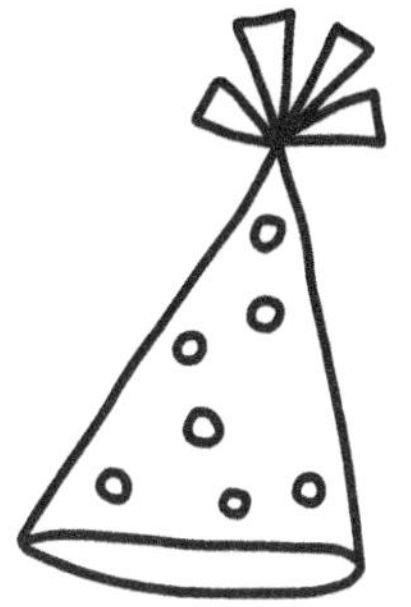

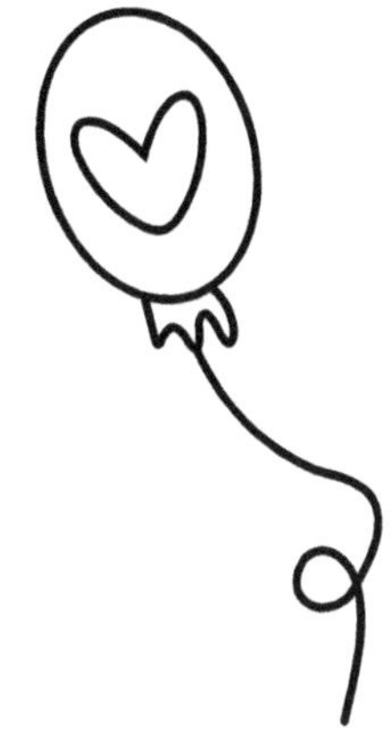

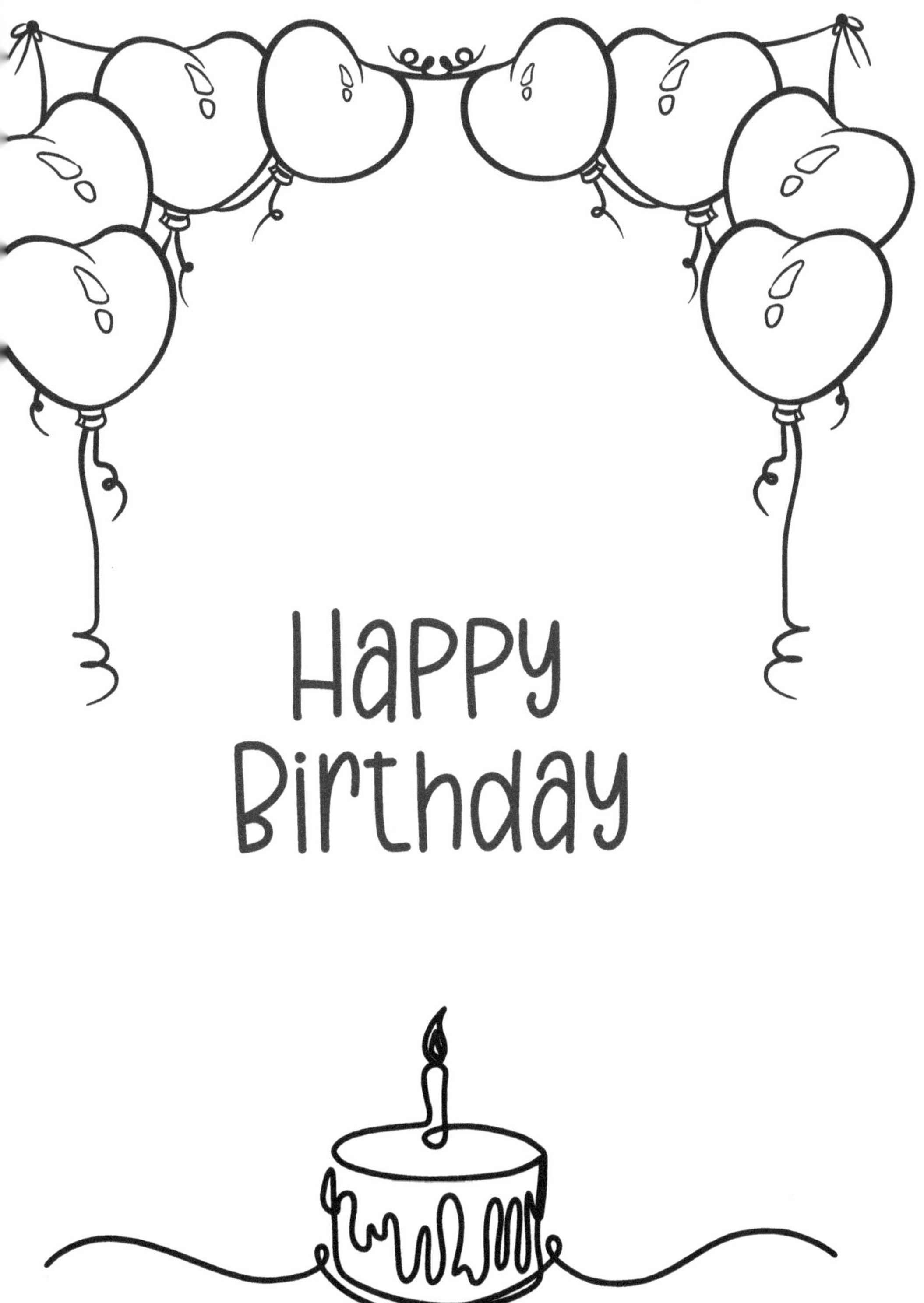
Happy
Birthday

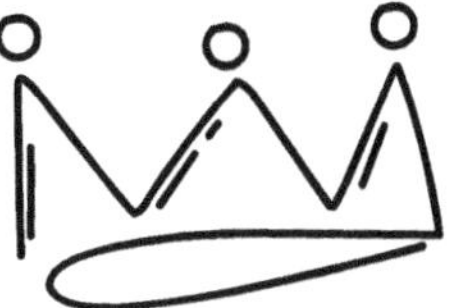

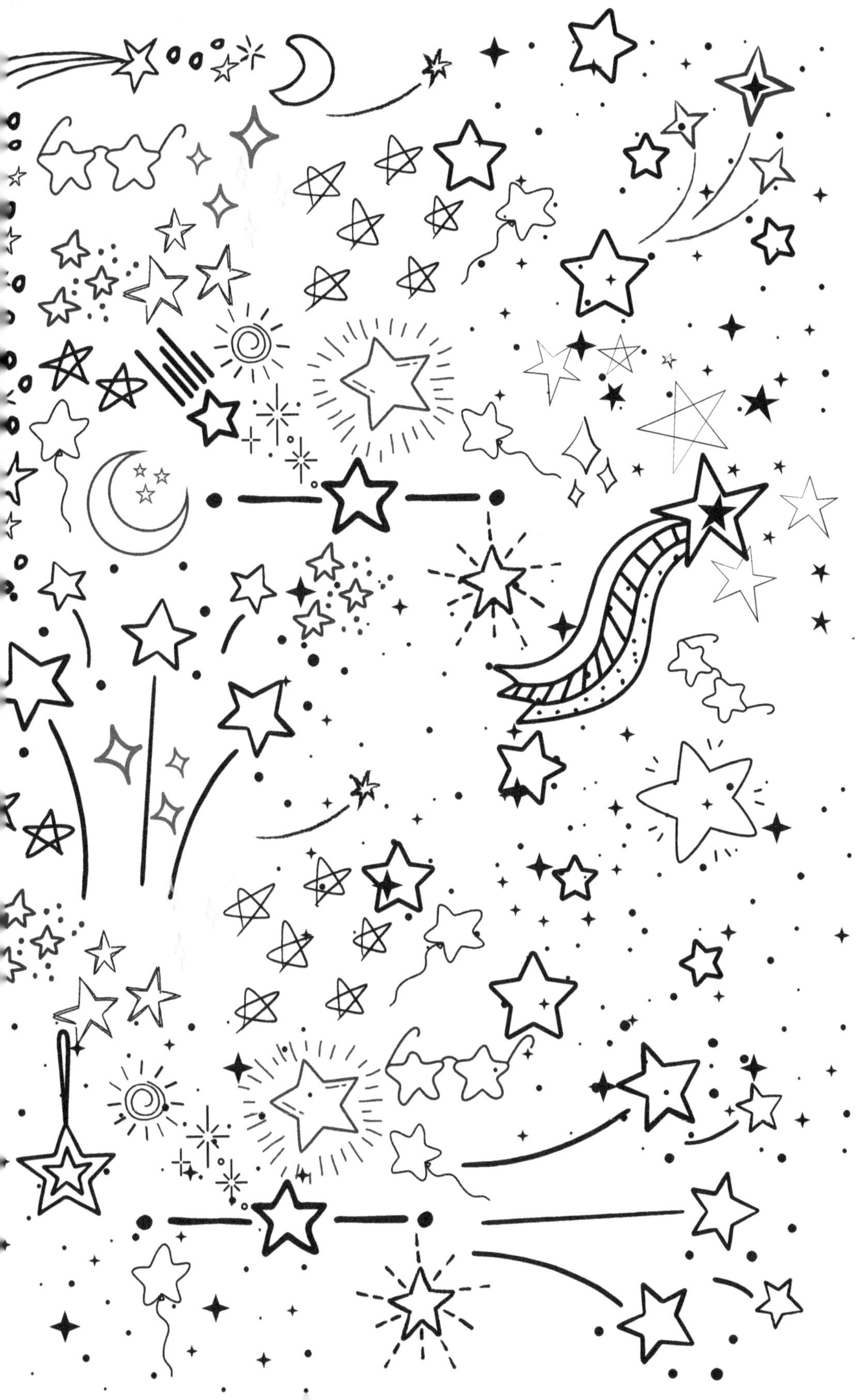

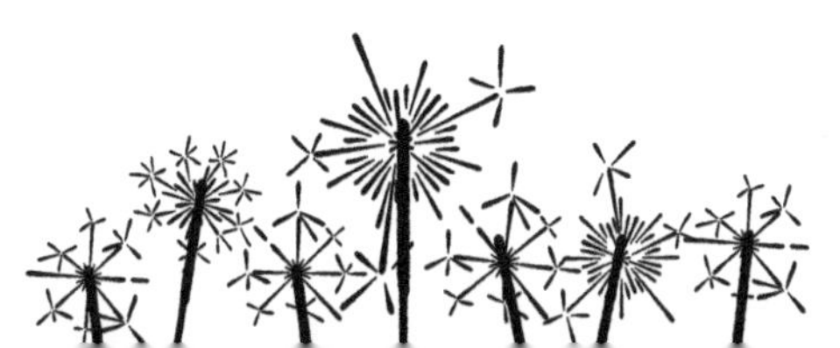

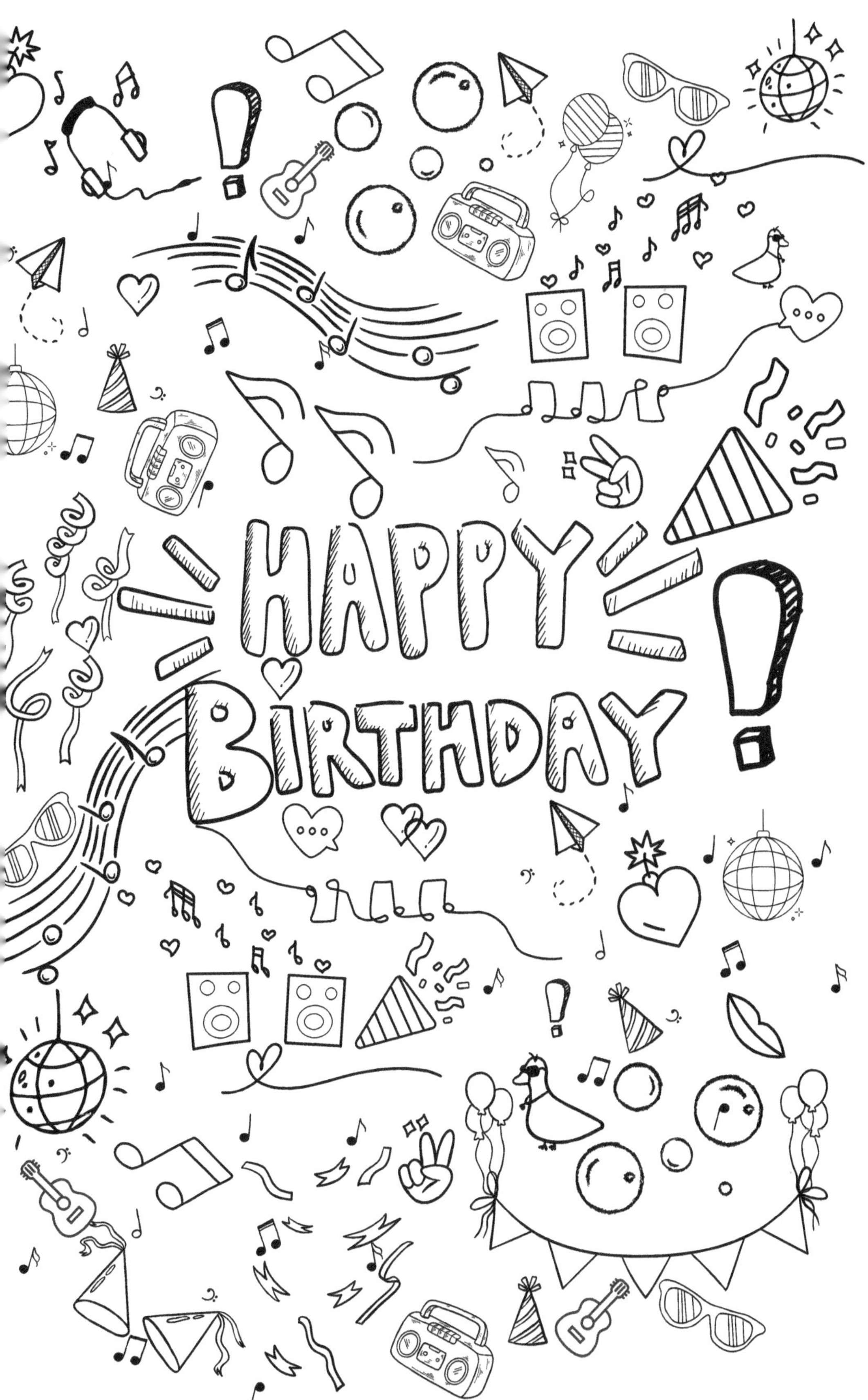

HAPPY
BIRTHDAY
!

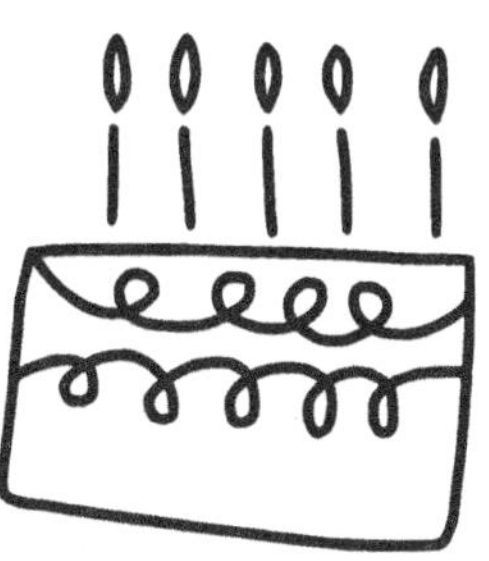

Wish List

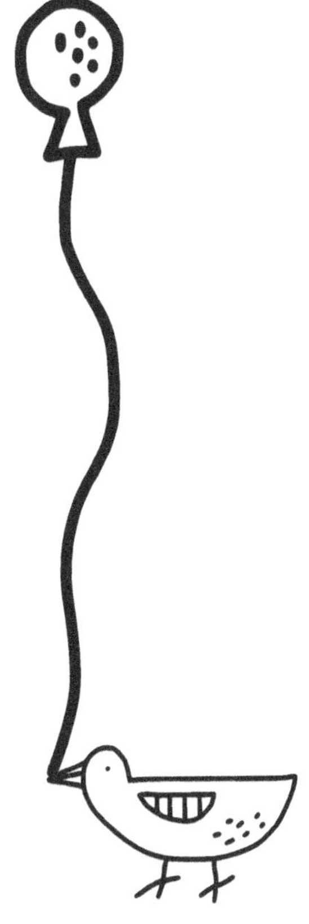

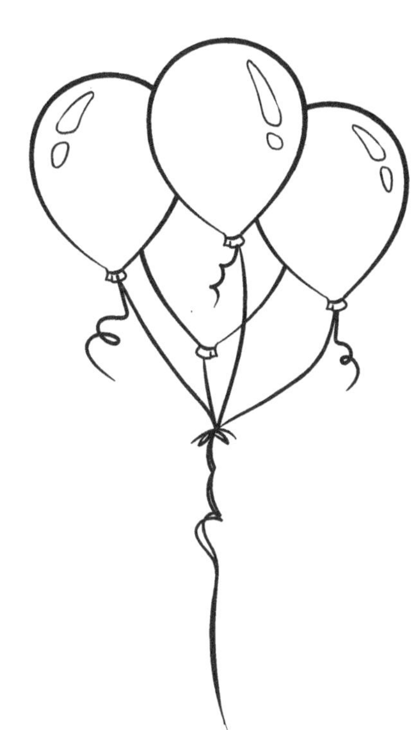

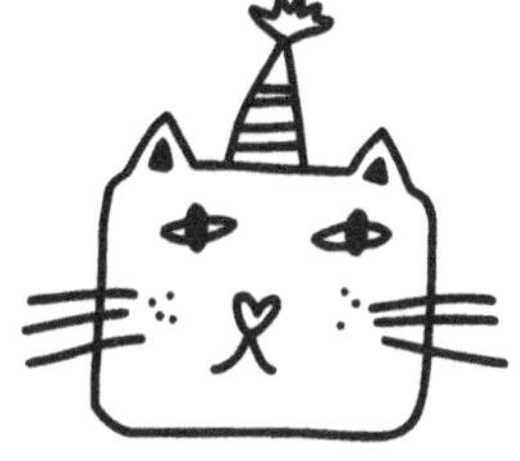

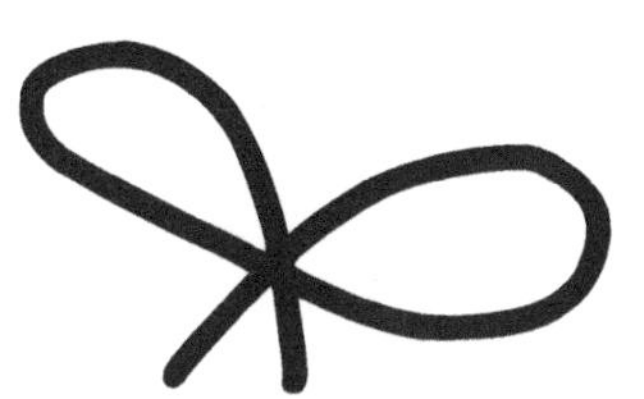

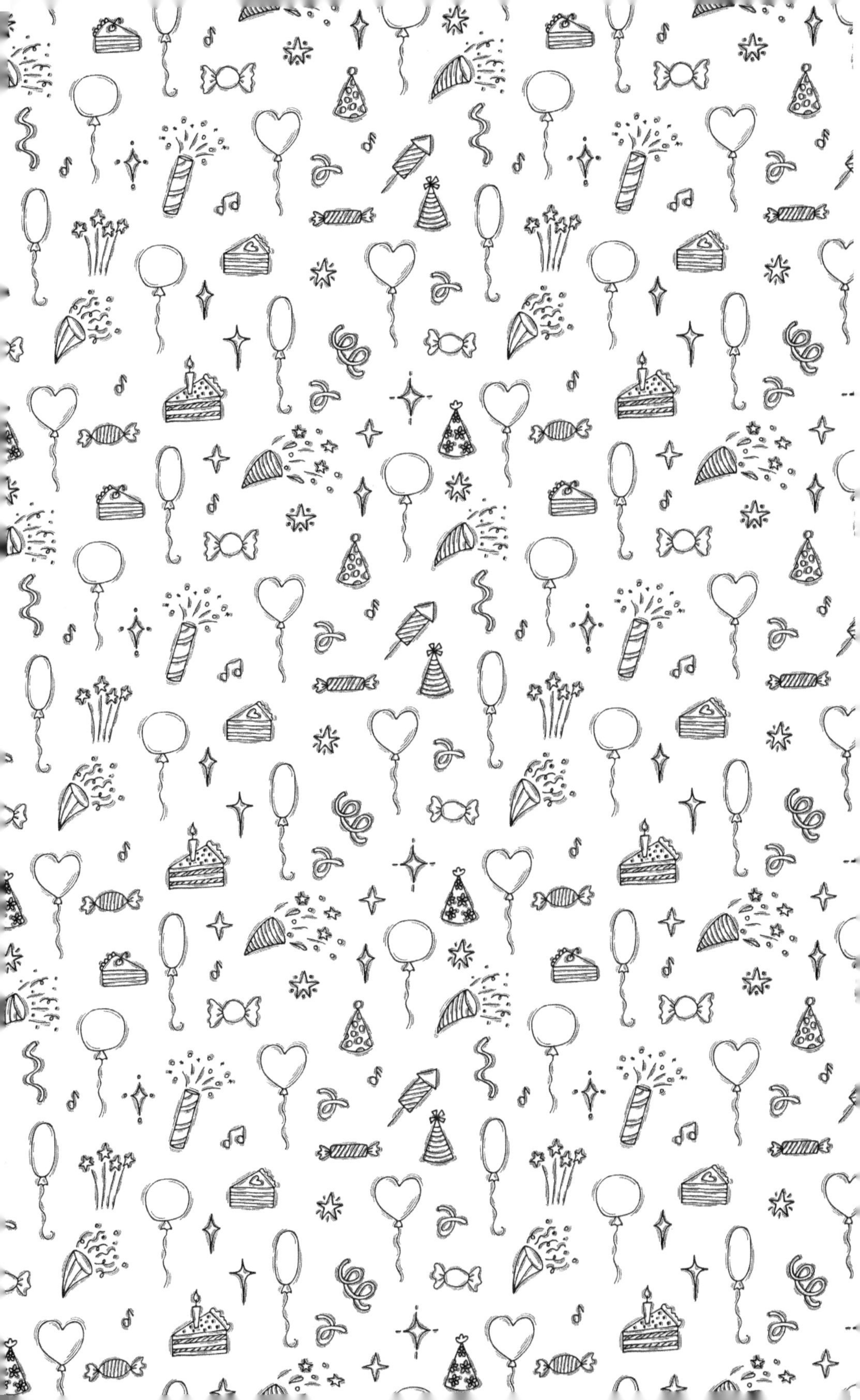

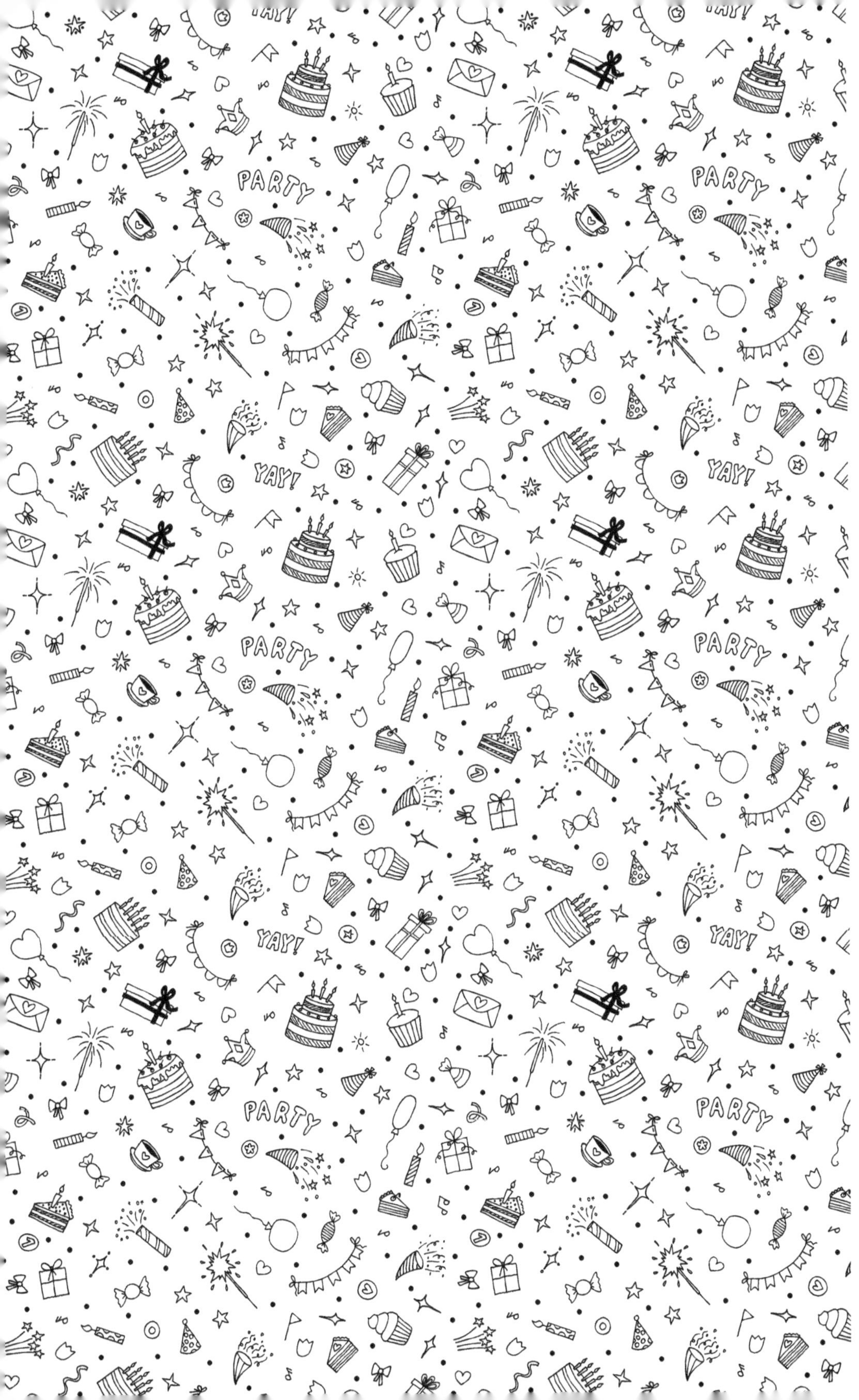

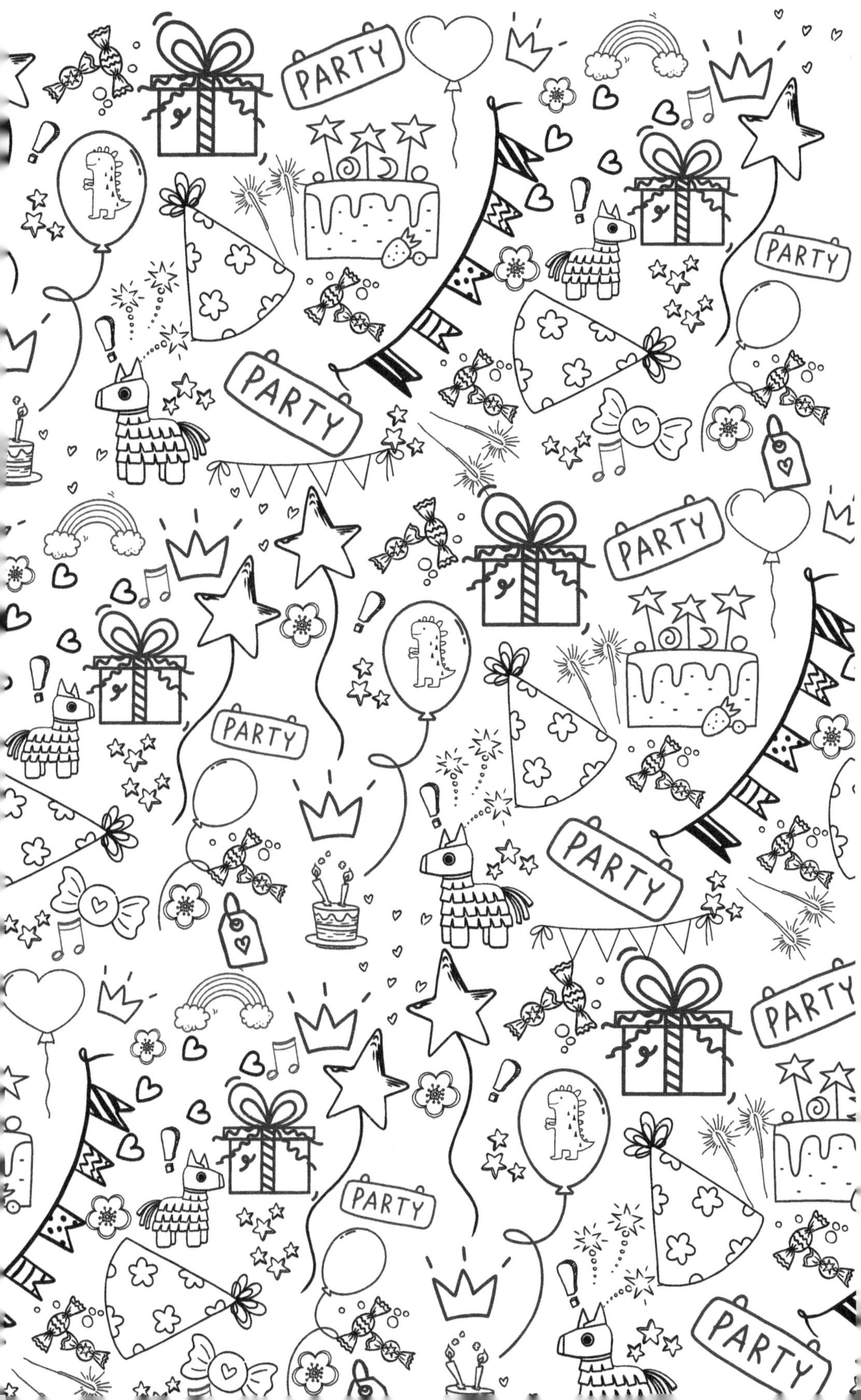

PARTY
PARTY
PARTY
PARTY
PARTY
PARTY
PARTY
PARTY

Happy Birthday to YOU!

Happy Birthday to YOU!

Happy Birthday to YOU!

Happy Birthday to YOU!

Happy Birthday to YOU!

Happy Birthday to YOU!

Happy Birthday to YOU!

Happy Birthday to YOU!

Happy Birthday to YOU!

Happy Birthday to YOU!

Happy Birthday to YOU!

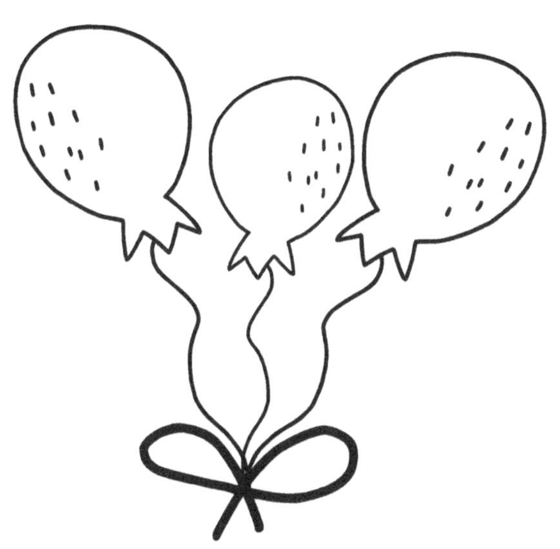

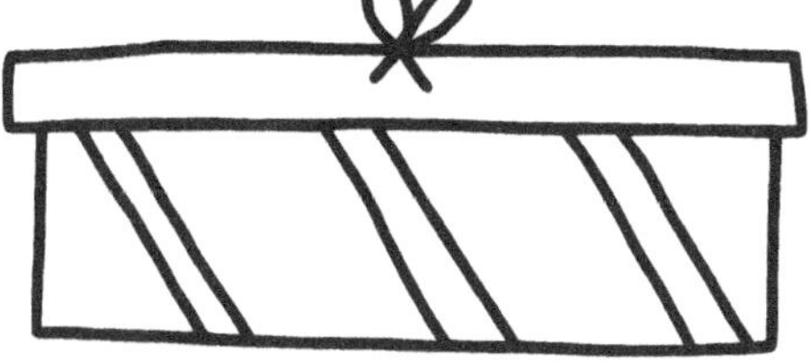

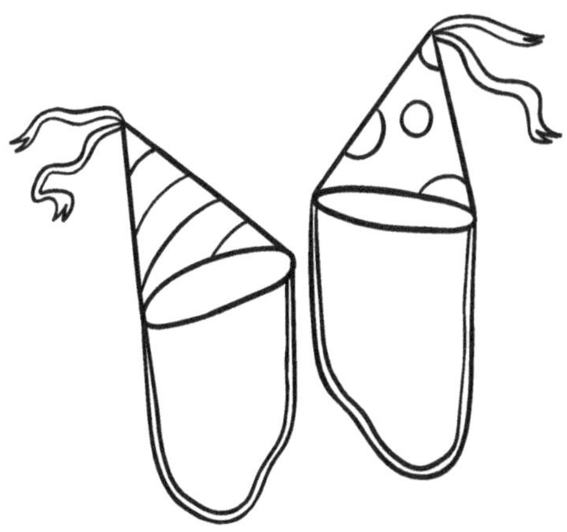

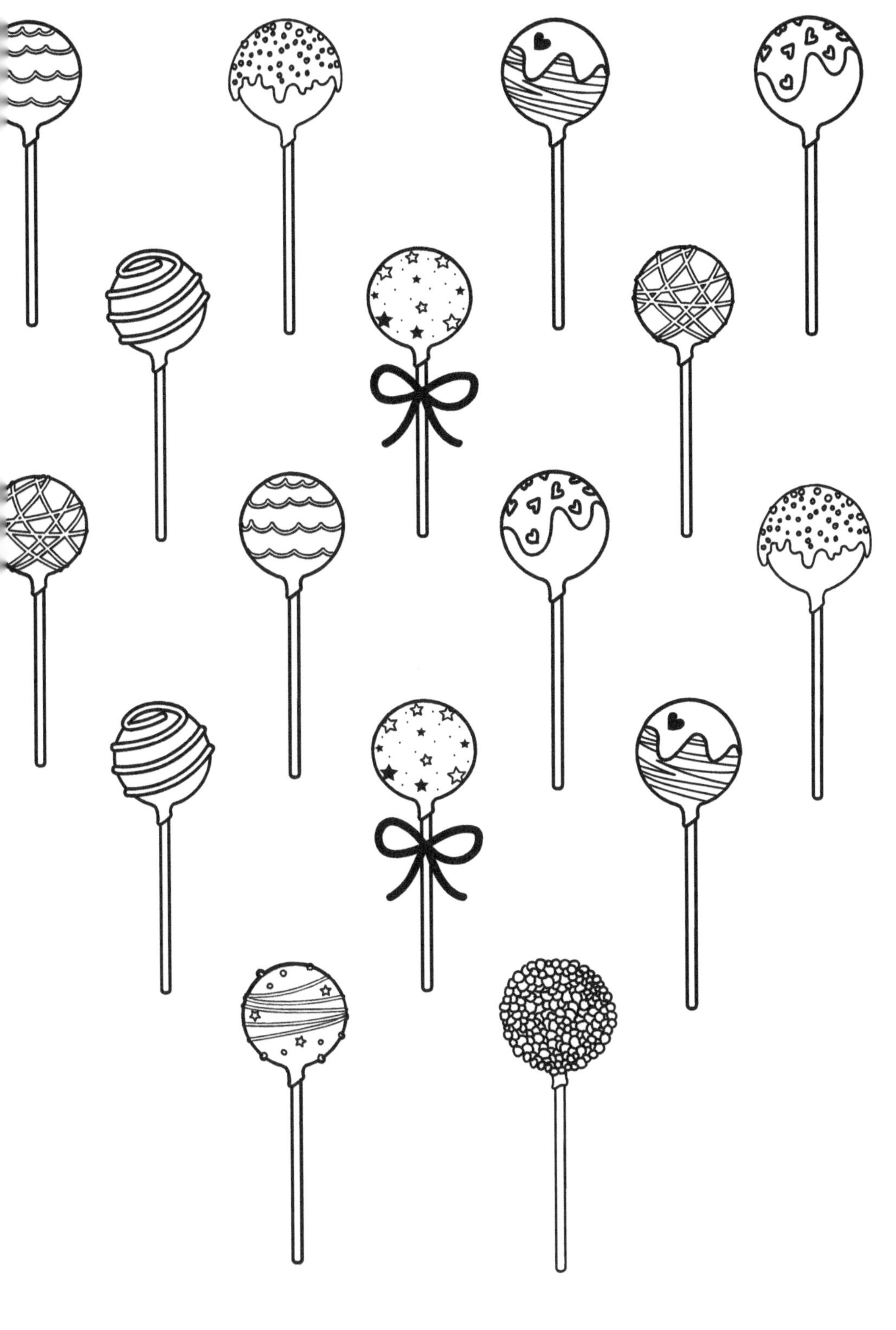

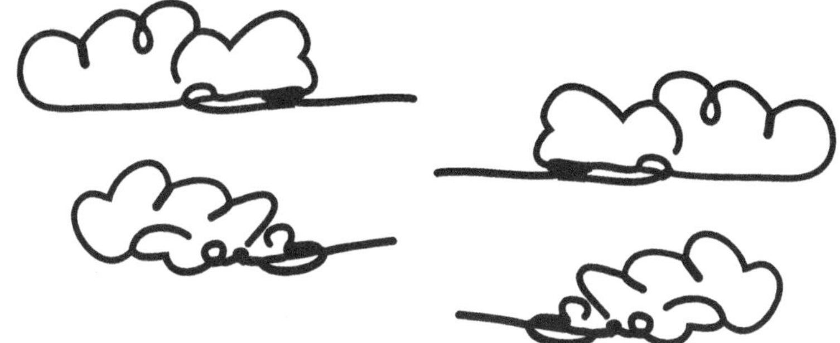

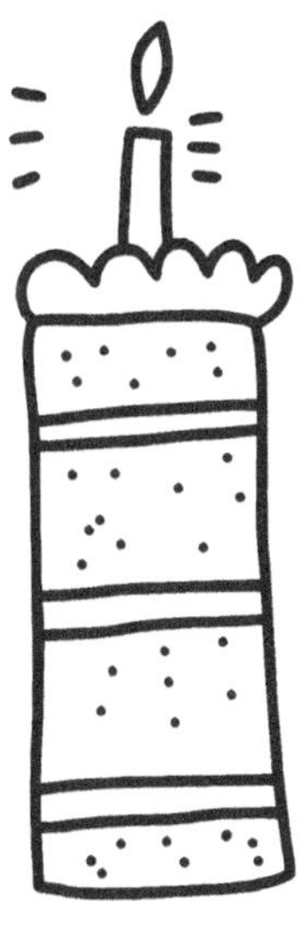

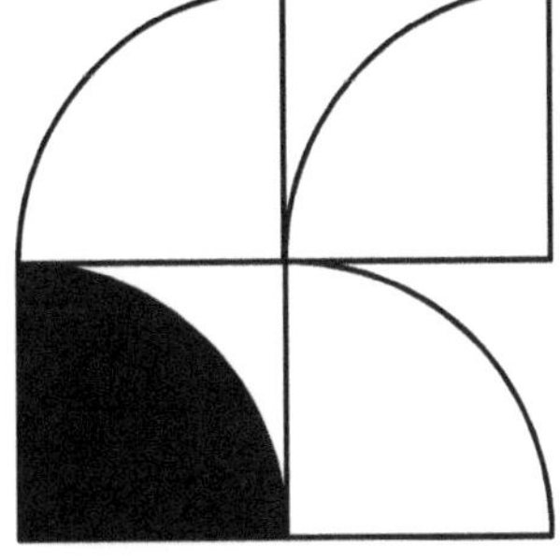

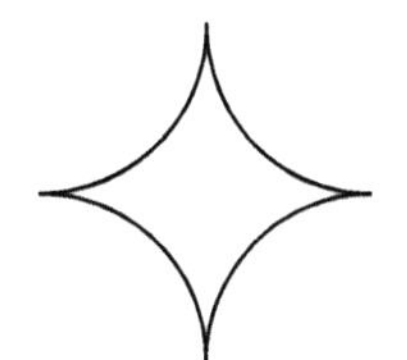

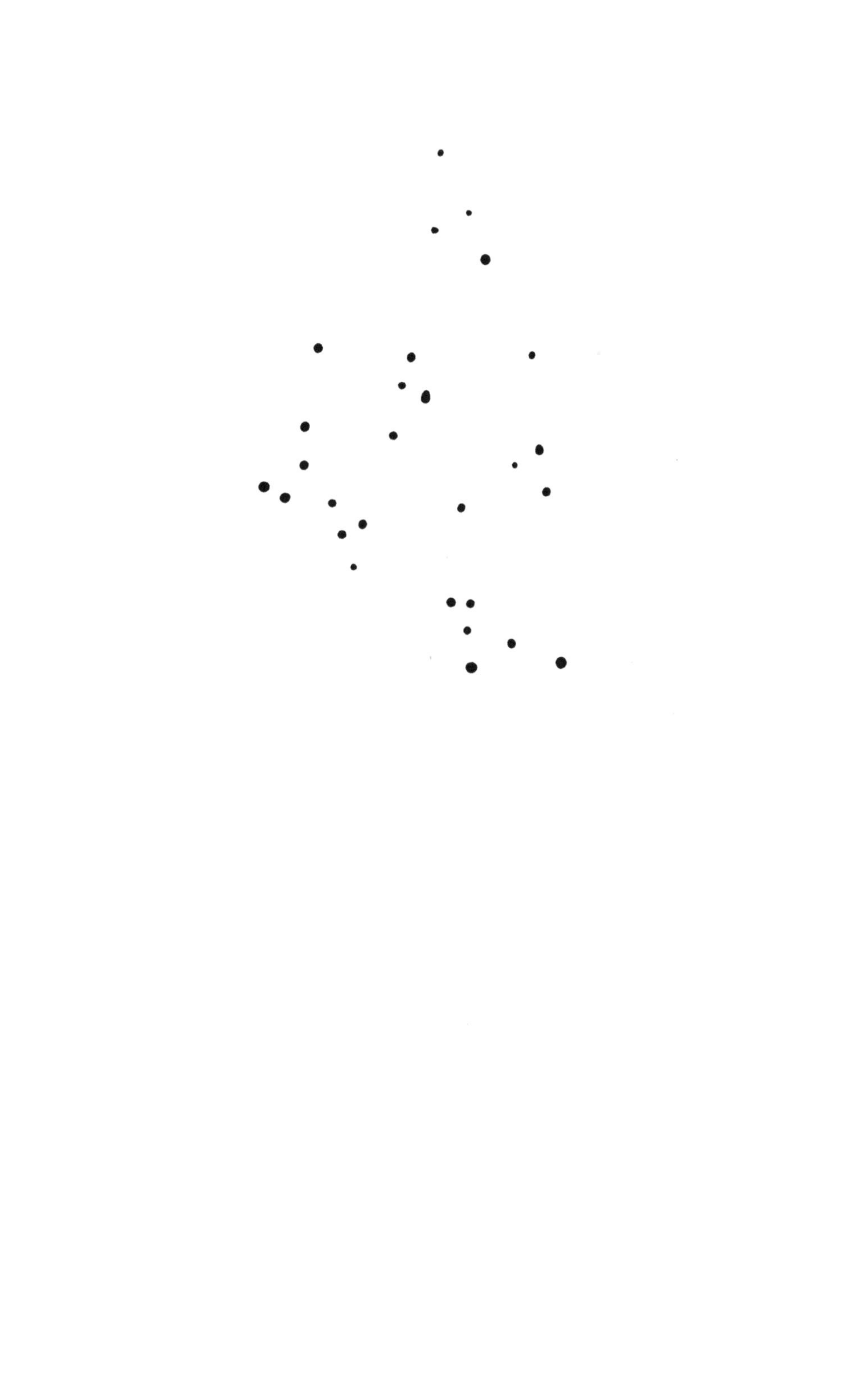

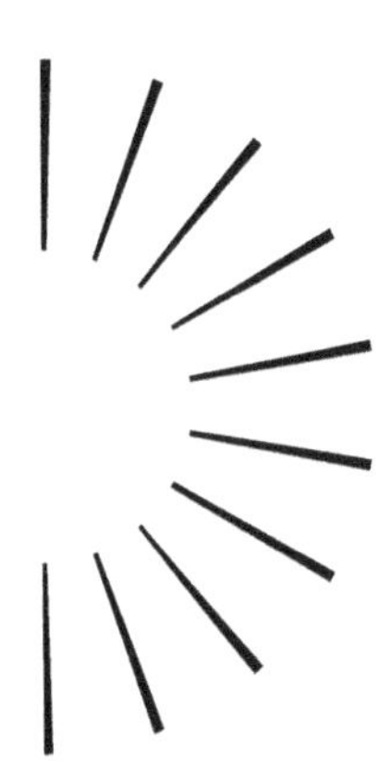

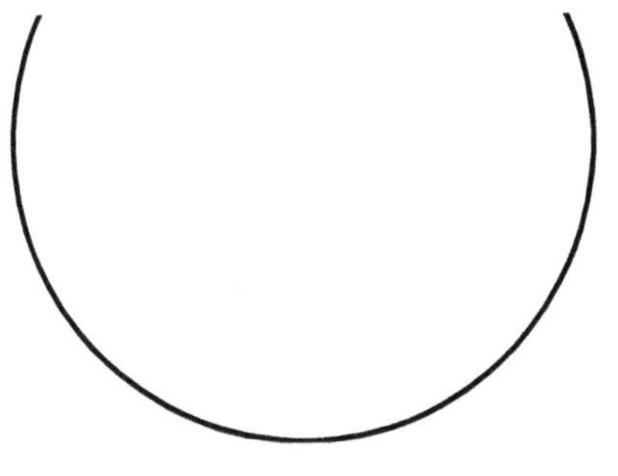

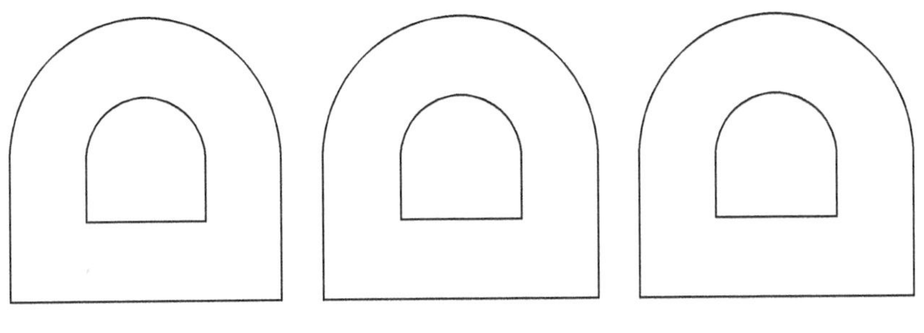

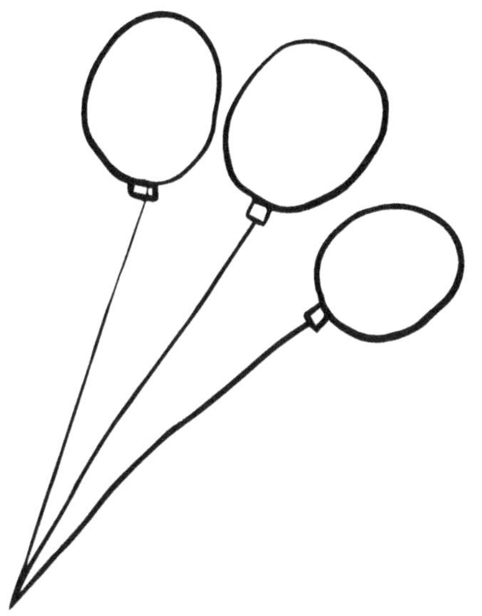

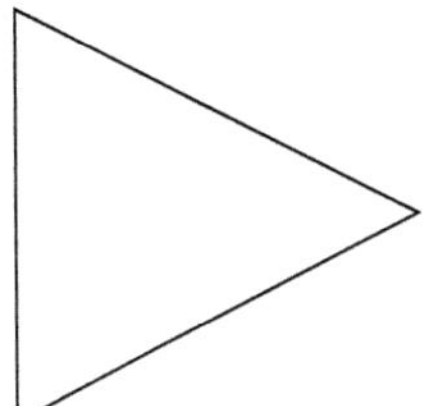

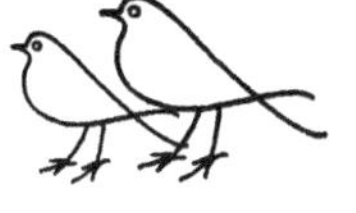
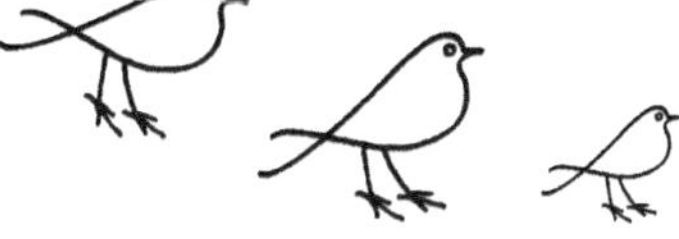

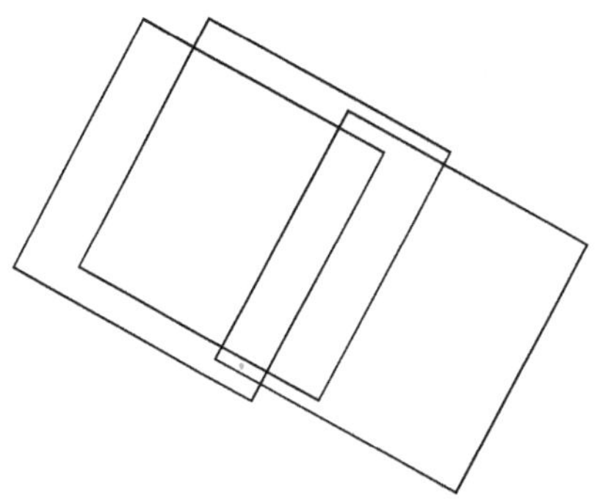

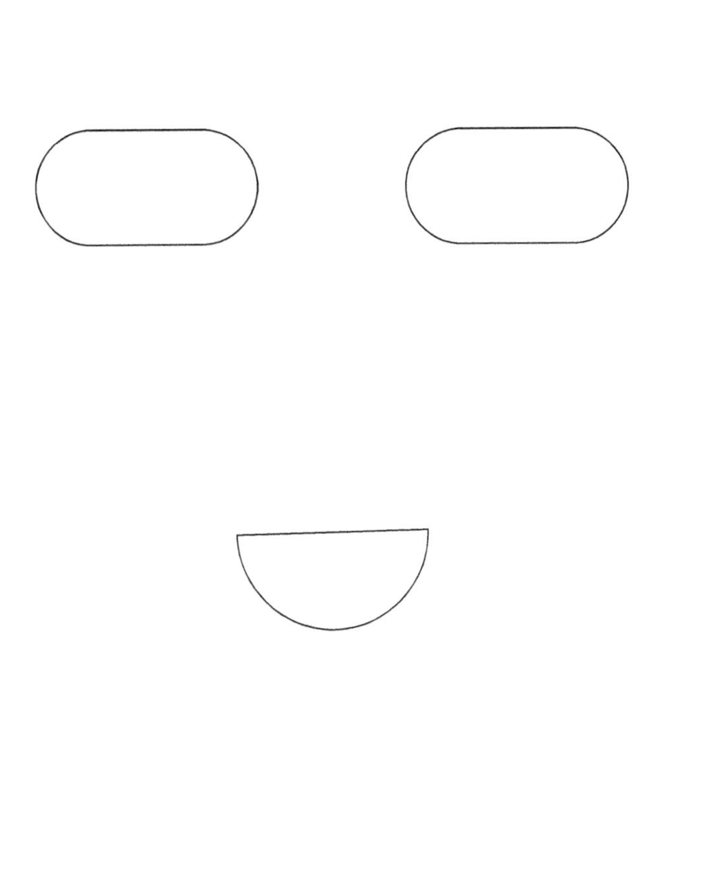

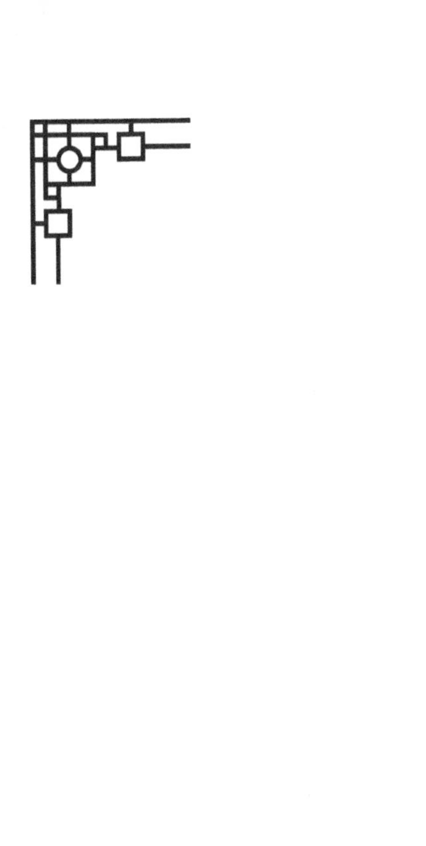

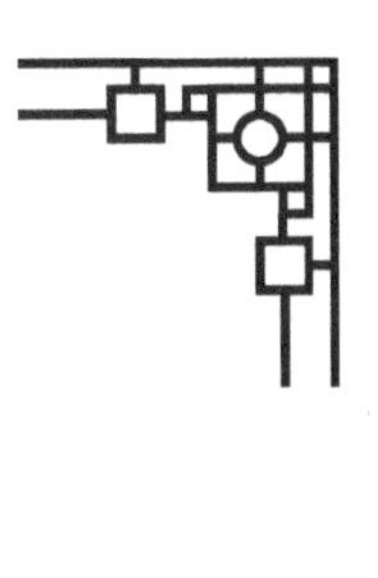

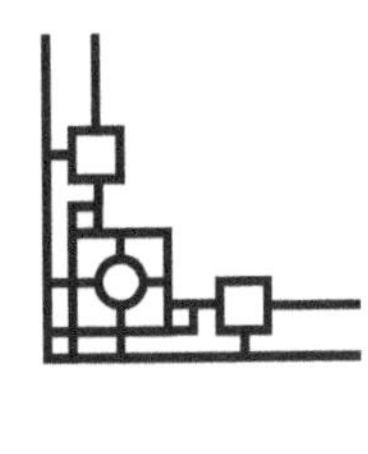
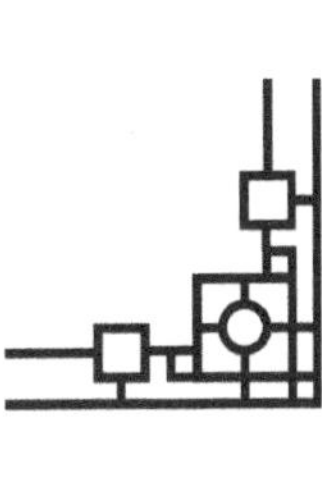

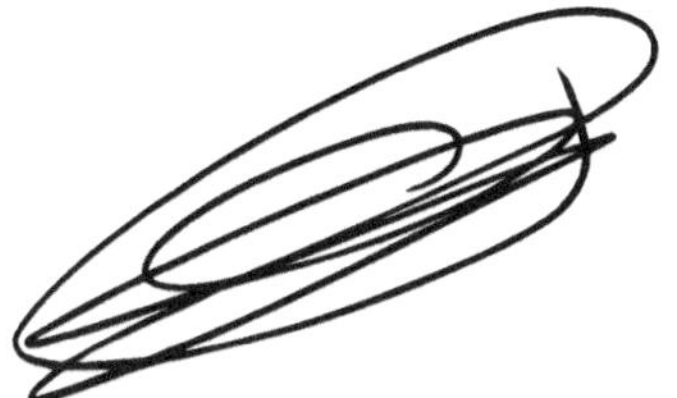

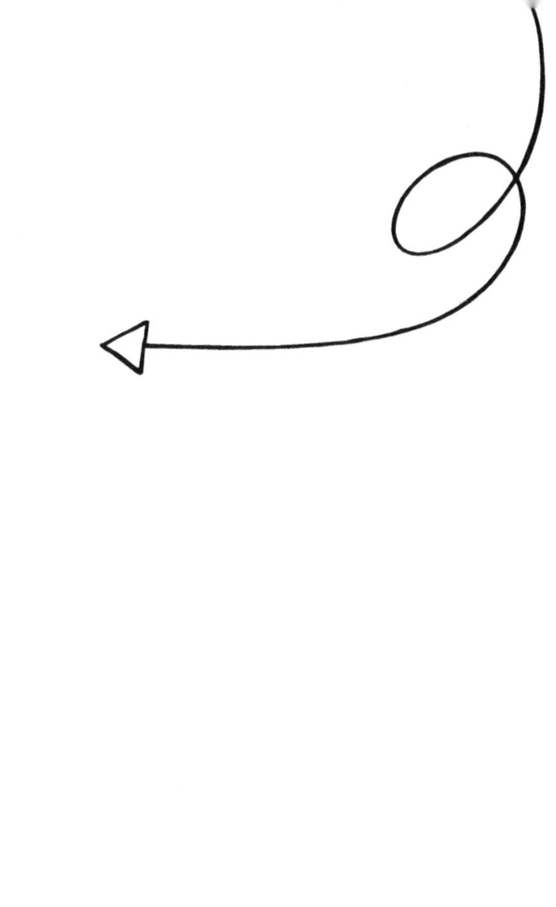

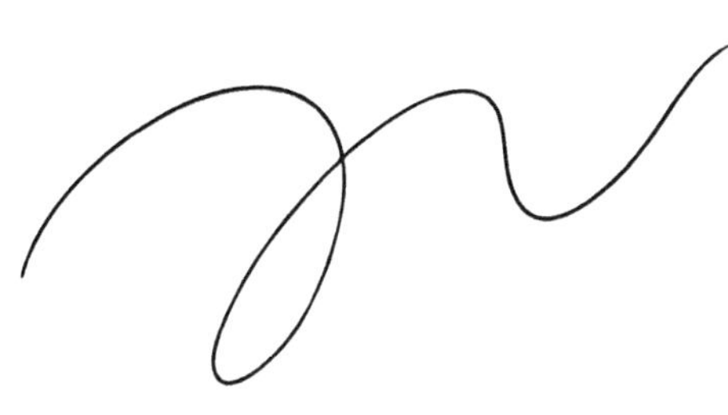

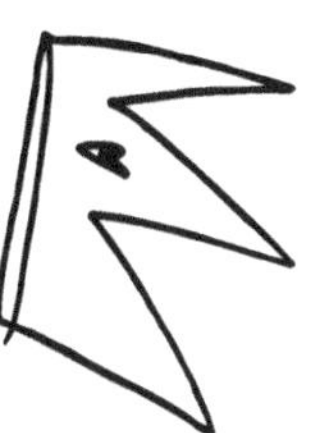
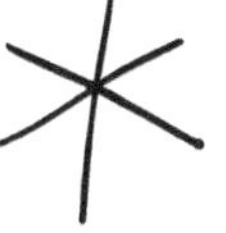
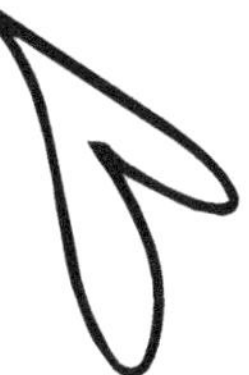

Bonus page:
Close your eyes and make a quick scribble on this page.
Now you have a new starter squiggle!

Bonus page:
Close your eyes and with your right hand make a quick scribble on this page.
Now you have a new starter squiggle!

Bonus page:
Close your eyes and with your left hand make a quick scribble on this page.
Now you have a new starter squiggle!

Bonus page:
Give someone else your pen, have them close their eyes and
make a quick scribble on this page.